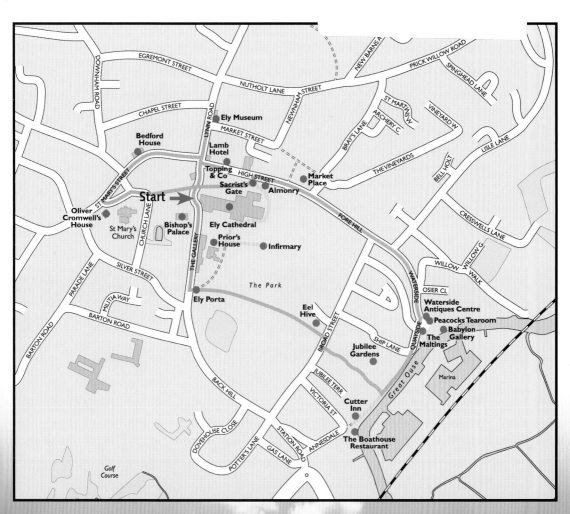

EGREMONT STREET

DOWNHAM ROAD

CHAPEL STREET

NUTHOLT LANE

NEWNHAM STREET

NEW BARNS A

PRICK WILLOW ROAD

SPINGHEAD LANE

LYNN ROAD

Ely Museum

MARKET STREET

ST MARTIN'S W

VINEYARD W

LISLE LANE

Bedford House

BRAY'S LANE

ARCHERY C

THE VINEYARDS

BELL HOLT

WILLOW G

Lamb Hotel

HIGH STREET

Topping & Co

Sacrist's Gate

Almonry

Market Place

ST MARY'S STREET

Start

CRESSWELLS LANE

Oliver Cromwell's House

Bishop's Palace

Ely Cathedral

FORE HILL

St Mary's Church

CHURCH LANE

Prior's House

Infirmary

THE GALLERY

WILLOW WALK

The Park

WATERSIDE

OSIER CL

Waterside Antiques Centre

SILVER STREET

Ely Porta

Peacocks Tearoom

PARADE LANE

MILITIA WAY

Eel Hive

QUAYSIDE

Babylon Gallery

The Maltings

BARTON ROAD

BROAD STREET

SHIP LANE

Jubilee Gardens

Great Ouse

Marina

BACK HILL

JUBILEE TERR.

VICTORIA ST

Cutter Inn

DOVEHOUSE CLOSE

POTTER'S LANE

STATION ROAD

GAS LANE

ANNESDALE

The Boathouse Restaurant

Golf Course

View across the Fens to Ely

Welcome to Ely

One of Britain's most exhilarating sights is to see from afar Ely's magnificent cathedral rising above the surrounding lowland. The ancient market town – a city, in effect, by virtue of this fine church – presides over the Fens: wide horizons of peaty farmland creating one of Britain's most fertile crop-growing areas. Ely's attractive streets wind down to where the River Great Ouse flows past, its willow-lined, duck-populated waterfront a charming complement to the architectural delights of the city.

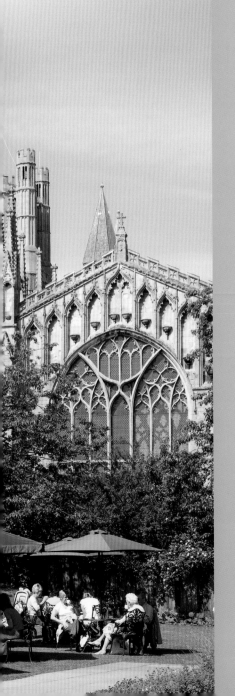

A short history

Early details of Ely's rich history are as mysterious as the impenetrable marshy Fenland wilderness that once surrounded the settlement. The hill on which the city grew was an isolated refuge from a land of water, reed and wind, and peopled by stubborn, self-sufficient folk known as the 'Fen tigers'.

The Romans were the first significant newcomers, around AD 100. To curb local resistance, they drained the land and built causeways, which fell into disrepair when they left.

In the 7th century, Etheldreda, daughter of an East Anglian king, built a priory in the Ely area. Marauding Danes destroyed it in 870, but by 1000 Ely was once again thriving: a small town with a rebuilt abbey, wealthy and powerful.

When the Normans tried to subdue the district, rebels, including one Hereward the Wake, came to Ely to resist, defying William the Conqueror's attempts to penetrate the Fens. Their presence burdened the monks, however, and in 1071 Abbot Thurstan secretly negotiated with the Normans, forcing Hereward to flee.

The potent symbol of William's rule was a new Norman cathedral on the hill. Medieval craftsmen and pilgrims to St Etheldreda's shrine brought prosperity to the town, further wealth came from the water: reeds (for thatching), fish – and eels which, it is thought, gave the city its name.

The Reformation brought an end to pilgrimage and serious damage to the cathedral's ornaments. The Civil War (1642–46) brought temporary closure to the cathedral when Oliver Cromwell, Puritan local MP and later Lord Protector of England, objected to the 'unedifying and offensive' chanting and inadequate short sermons. Around this time, the Fens began to be drained in earnest, greatly to the detriment of the Fen tigers.

In 1816 at nearby Littleport there were riots, the worst in the country, in protest against low wages and high prices (see page 13). The arrival of the railway in 1845 brought new prosperity to the town. Although many old industries have gone, new businesses have replaced them, and Ely is now one of the fastest-growing cities in the country, thriving as a cultural community, tourist centre and dormitory town for Cambridge and London.

Ely Cathedral

The 'ship of the Fens' is one of the marvels of the medieval world. A large part of the cathedral was built nearly a thousand years ago; almost all the newer elements are around seven centuries old. With one brief interruption (see panel below), worship has gone on in this building every day since AD 1106, a remarkable fact in itself.

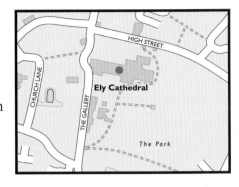

Mixed motives

In 1643 Parliamentary soldiers had wrecked the interior of Peterborough Cathedral in a Puritan reaction against the ornamentation associated with the outlawed Catholic religion. In Ely, Cromwell ordered cathedral clergy to suspend services, enforcing this with soldiers when they disobeyed. One theory has it that he did this to prevent similar destruction in his 'home' cathedral.

What the Normans did

Between 1083 and 1189 the Normans built a mighty new cathedral, with Northamptonshire limestone paid for in eels, in their classic round-arch style, known as Romanesque. Although building began at the east (altar) end, the main transepts are the oldest surviving areas of the church. This is because, by 1252, the east end was rebuilt in the new Gothic style to make room for the hordes of pilgrims who flocked to St Etheldreda's shrine. Furthermore, in 1322 the original tower collapsed, later to be replaced by the structurally unique octagon.

The cathedral from the park

The nave

Apart from the superb Norman arcading, the nave is notable for its fine Victorian stained-glass windows, depicting Bible stories in attractive vivid colours. One of its other glories is the unusual painted ceiling, designed and begun in 1858 by Henry Styleman Le Strange and completed, on his death, by his friend Thomas Gambier Parry. In order to paint the ceiling, the men had to lie for many hours on their backs in very poor light.

Tower of Babel window in the nave aisle

Gargoyle on the exterior

West end

This was the last part of the original building to be completed, illustrated by the appearance of the Gothic style in several places, notably the lovely Galilee porch by which you enter the cathedral, added in 1215. The original west front was even more magnificent than it is today. Then, it had two transepts of its own, and colourful statues in its niches. Unfortunately, the north-west transept fell, or was pulled, down, never to be replaced. This was probably a side effect of the weighty octagonal belfry added to the Norman tower in 1392.

Transepts

The main transepts provide the cathedral's 'cross' shape. From the original building, they too have rounded Norman windows and arches. Unfortunately, rubble-filled cavities made the walls less strong than they look and, over the years, they became a source of anxiety to cathedral architects. Evidence of rebuilding can be seen in the Gothic-style topmost windows and the 15th-century hammerbeam roofs. The faded wall paintings in St Edmund's Chapel (off the south transept) are a reminder that the stone and plaster of medieval cathedrals were originally ablaze with colour.

Ely Cathedral

The octagon and lantern

The octagon

The collapse of the cathedral's central bell tower on the night of 12 February 1322 literally shook the town. The unique structure that replaced it is an engineering masterpiece. It is the pinnacle of achievement in a treasure house filled with work of the highest order, executed to the glory of God and a tribute to the creativity of mankind.

After the tower had fallen, the span was considered too wide for heavy stone vaulting to fill it. So Alan de Walsingham, the cathedral's sacrist (administrator), came up with the ground-breaking idea of an octagonal space. The king's master carpenter, William Hurley, devised a timber structure to make his vision a reality. From an octagonal platform of eight huge tree trunks, long triangular bracing timbers supported a lantern, clad in lead. Constructing the octagon took six years, the lantern 14. The sculptures below it chart the life of St Etheldreda; the Victorian paintings on the doors below the windows depict angels.

Choir and presbytery

At 5.30 on most evenings, everyone is welcome to sit in the ancient choir stalls and listen to the choir sing Evensong, a wonderful and timeless experience. It also offers a good opportunity to appreciate the art of the medieval carver. Behind the stalls, the 14th-century stone arches are in the elaborate Decorated style. Towards the altar (the area called the presbytery) the style is Early English and generally plainer. The aisles behind the choir contain many superb monuments.

Lady Chapel

Most medieval English cathedrals have chapels dedicated to the Virgin Mary, but Ely's is special. It is the largest of its kind in any British cathedral, with the widest stone vault (ceiling) of its day. It is, unusually, attached to the north choir aisle, not at the east end as in most other cathedrals. In medieval times it would have been far darker, a mass of coloured stonework and stained glass. The glass and the colour were eliminated at the Reformation. Until 1938, the chapel served as the town's parish church.

Two chantry chapels

Beyond the Presbytery are two superb chantries representing the height of magnificence in Gothic architecture. Chantries are chapels where prayers were said for the souls of the dead who lie within them, in this case two Bishops of Ely, Alcock (died 1500) and West (died 1534). Despite damage during the Reformation, the carving of ceilings, screens and canopies is breathtaking and shouldn't be missed.

Jonathan Clarke's 'The Way of Life'

'Christus' by Hans Feibusch

Art in the cathedral

Ely has many modern examples of superb creativity. Among them, at the west end, *Christus* by Hans Feibusch (1981) welcomes visitors with open arms. Soaring up the nearby wall of the former north-west transept is *The Way of Life* by Jonathan Clarke (2001). Its nine aluminium sections show the unpredictable journey of faith. Look for the tiny human near the top. In the south transept is a David Wynne sculpture (1967) showing the Easter encounter between Jesus and Mary Magdalene.

Gurney stoves

The Victorian cast-iron stoves seen around Ely Cathedral were once present in many churches around the land, and are now a rarity. Invented by Goldsworthy Gurney in 1856, they burned anthracite or coke and had a tray of water beneath them to moisten the atmosphere. Ely's gurneys are now converted to gas, controlled electronically.

Stained Glass Museum

Stained glass has been adding vivid colour to English cathedrals, churches and castles for almost a thousand years. Britain's only stained-glass museum, housed in the south gallery of Ely Cathedral, traces the history of stained glass and shows how it is made. Uniquely, it gives us a chance to study, at close quarters, a national collection of beautiful and important examples of this superb art form.

St Wilfrid and St John Berchmans

The work of Harry Clarke (1889–1931) is important for its innovative and intricate jewelled technique. The 1927 window of which the picture (right) is a detail was originally installed in a Glasgow convent for trainee women teachers. St Wilfrid (c.634–710) encouraged St Etheldreda to devote herself to her religious life in Ely, while St John Berchmans (1599–1621), a Belgian Jesuit, is the patron saint of young people. Clarke's death at 42 is thought to have been hastened by fumes from the acid used in the etching of his stained glass.

Detail of window depicting St Wilfrid and St John Berchmans

Stamped quarry

The medieval glass that survives in some of Britain's cathedrals often includes quarries painted with images of birds, flowers or leaves. Victorian copies, exhibited at the museum, were made by rolling or pressing soft glass into patterned moulds. Then pigment and/or stain was applied to the indented pattern before firing.

Bust of a King

In the museum there is a figure of a royal saint or Old Testament king which is around 800 years old. It comes from Soissons Cathedral in France, a landmark building in the development of the Gothic style, and one of the first to include windows such as this.

Prodigal Son

The panel depicting various episodes from the popular parable of the prodigal son was created in 1930 when Moira Forsyth (1905–91) was a student at the Royal College of Art. It captures perfectly the spirit and humour of the age. With windows in Eton College and various cathedrals, Forsyth became one of Britain's most respected stained-glass artists.

'Prodigal Son' by Moira Forsyth

'Bust of a King'

Face of My Father

James Powell & Sons (1720–1980) was Britain's longest-running glass house, their 'Whitefriars' designs always reflecting the fashion of the day and often setting the trend themselves. *Face of My Father* comes from a classically Victorian example, made in 1892 for a London church. It was the work of J.W. Brown, the company's leading stained-glass designer.

Stained Glass Museum

Cathedral precincts

Ely's monastery was founded by Etheldreda in AD 673. In 1109 a bishopric was created, with the monastery, by now very wealthy, run by a prior instead of an abbot. Much of the cathedral is Norman but many of its monastic buildings came later, added in a whirl of new construction, extension and alteration, which continued through the Middle Ages until the Dissolution of the Monasteries of 1539.

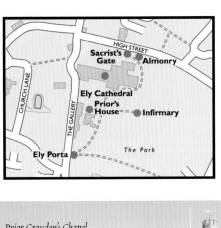

Prior Crauden's Chapel

Prior's House

Prior's House

Part of a prior's duty was to provide hospitality for important guests. Judging by the many additions to the Prior's House, the demands must have changed significantly over the years. The earliest part, begun late in the 12th century, is the small hall with its fine undercroft, remodelled twice in the next 400 years. A bigger hall was demolished at the Reformation. The Queen's Hall, behind the house and fronting The Gallery, was guest accommodation. It is now part of King's School. Pride of place in the complex goes to Prior Crauden's Chapel, a highly decorated place for private prayer, built for Prior John of Crauden by 1325.

Ely Porta

Ely Porta

This is the cathedral's largest surviving gate, begun in 1397, a few years after Ely merchants had stormed the cathedral in protest against the power of the bishop. The Porta provided sturdy protection to the abbey precincts and also served the cause of justice. Thus, prisoners detained in the cell on the ground floor would be tried in the courthouse above. Next to the Porta is the monastic barn, with its magnificent medieval roof of exposed wooden beams, once used for storing the monastery's grain but now serving as the dining hall of King's School.

Two fine doors

The cloisters, with their four covered walkways and central lawn (garth), were the hub of the monastery, where monks would walk, talk, study and teach. Sadly, little remains of Ely's cloisters. Important survivals, though, are the two doors that linked monastery and church. One is the Monks' Door through which monks processed; the grander of the two is the Prior's Door, where the abbey's civilian guests once entered the church. Above, its stone tympanum shows Christ in Judgement, reminding those who pass beneath of the inevitable day of reckoning.

Infirmary

This building, originating in the 12th century, was primarily where monks would go when sick, or to retire. It was also the scene of regular blood-letting, using leeches – once considered an essential part of healthy living. Long and rectangular, it was built on similar lines to a church with a nave, chancel and aisles. Today's Firmary Lane was once the roofed hall, with the arcading still visible at the sides. The adjacent 'Black Hostelry' was where visiting Benedictine monks, in their black habits, would stay.

Stonework over the Prior's Door

Tradesman's entrance

The sacrist supervised the buildings and supplied the cathedral's many altars – anything from collecting salt for the holy water to looking after the cemetery. The 1325 building, which housed his bustling headquarters, still stands on the High Street. The Sacrist's Gate (pictured on page 30), once the tradesman's entrance to the cathedral's yards and workshops, passes beneath it. The Almonry, now a tea room in the same row of buildings, linked the monastery and community, for here food was given to the poor and the town's children were educated.

Ely Museum

This lively little museum offers a journey through time, telling the story of Ely and the Fens from prehistoric days to the present and giving excellent background and context for visitors to the city.

Early Ely

Three of the museum's galleries have artefacts left by early inhabitants. One of the oldest is a mammoth's jawbone from 10,000 years ago. Much later are tools from flint mined in Norfolk and perhaps traded for eels by the Fen people. There is a copy of a Roman helmet from Stonea near March, and a beautiful Saxon gold ring. The museum also tells the story of St Etheldreda's 600-mile (965-kilometre) journey, pursued by an angry husband, before she founded the monastery in Ely.

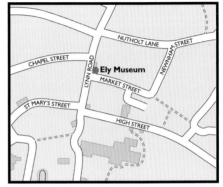

Ancient boneshakers

The Fens

Gallery 5 shows the pleasure and pain of pre-drainage Fenland life. All sorts of local tools are displayed, including metal gleeves (elsewhere called glaives) – gruesome-looking three-pronged spears used to catch elusive eels. The story is told of how the Earl of Bedford employed Cornelius Vermuyden to drain the Fens, sacrificing the livelihoods of local folk in favour of 'Gentlemen Adventurers', 17th-century 'fat cats' who funded the transformation in search of big profits (which often failed to materialize).

Eels and more eels

Eels were a great medieval delicacy and at that time 27,000 eels per year were harvested at nearby Doddington, and 24,000 at Stuntney. The monks of Ely paid for the masonry to expand their monastery by delivering eels straight from their ponds to the kitchens of their fellow monks at Peterborough Abbey.

Bishop's Gaol

For 150 years, the building that now houses the museum was the Bishop's Gaol. Its cruel past is revived in Gallery 7 – the condemned cell has lifelike inhabitants. Wellington's victory over Napoleon at Waterloo cost England dear: simply, the poor starved to pay for the troops. On 22 May 1816, rioting spread to nearby Littleport. 'Give us a living wage!' was the cry. The militia brought 86 rioters to Ely's gaol to await trial. The cells were cold and damp; food and bedding were sold, but only to those who could afford it; sanitary conditions were dreadful; misbehaviour was dealt with ruthlessly. Five rioters were hanged, some imprisoned, others transported to Australia.

The gaol gallery

Not really a criminal!

Ely in the last two centuries

Fenland peat yielded fine barley, and Ely became famous for its beer – in 1900 the town had 60 pubs and four breweries. Eventually the four were whittled down to one, owned by Watney Mann, at the bottom of Fore Hill. A fire in its malthouse closed it in 1967. Although the brewery was demolished, the malthouse survives as The Maltings (see page 21). Other displays tell, for example, of Ely's 40 basketmakers as well as the former leather and sugar beet industries; also how wildfowlers went about their crafty business with decoys, nets and punt guns.

The Victorian parlour

Oliver Cromwell's House

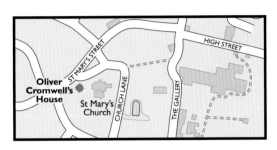

The name of Oliver Cromwell is one of the most famous in English history. A local man with limited ambitions, he emerged in the Civil War as a brilliant Parliamentary general. Through a strong sense of God's calling, he had greatness thrust upon him, ruling as Lord Protector during the Commonwealth of 1653–58, when England became a republic for a few short years.

St Mary's Church and Cromwell's House

Cromwell and Ely

Born in Huntingdon in 1599, Cromwell went to Cambridge University, married in 1620 and lived at St Ives, where he and his wife, Elizabeth, started a family of eight children. In 1628 he became a Member of Parliament and in 1636 he inherited a large estate from his uncle, Sir Thomas Steward, who lived at Stuntney outside Ely. Part of the legacy was the house next to St Mary's Church and the post of 'farmer of the tithes' whose duties included collecting money, wheat and straw on behalf of the Dean and Chapter of Ely. His (unwanted) nickname was 'Lord of the Fens'.

Cromwell and his house

Cromwell, Elizabeth and their children lived in the house from 1636 until not long before the Civil War broke out in 1642. Elizabeth and the children remained until 1647 and Cromwell's last two children, Frances and Mary, were born here. The house itself is much older, dating from around 1215. Behind the dark oak walls of the first room one visits, just inside the entrance, are fine examples of early painted panelling dating from 1572.

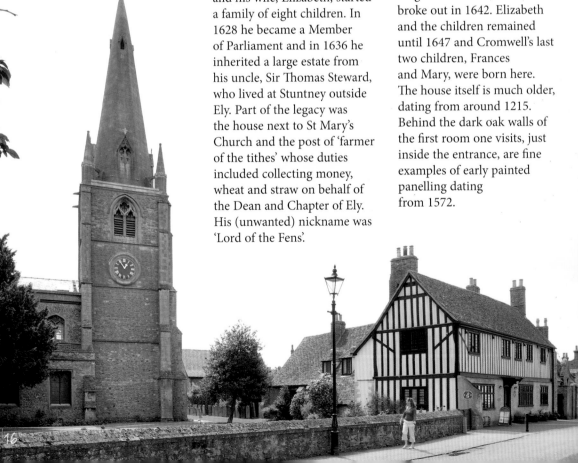

Modern Cromwelliana

If you're heading to Newmarket on the A142, look out on the left as you near the village of Stuntney. Here, on the site where Cromwell's mother was born and his uncle, Sir Thomas Steward, lived, a private owner has built a modern home in a 'retro' style similar to that of the original dwelling, which was allowed to fall into decay.

The kitchen

The kitchen

The east wing, the oldest part of the house, was once much bigger, serving as a hall for the collection and storage of tithes. The huge 15th-century fireplace was the hub of the house, by no means just for warmth. Here all the cooking went on; bread was baked in side ovens set into the chimney; meat might be boiled with vegetables tied in cloth, or roasted on a hand-turned spit. The Cromwells, who had known hard times, preferred plain food and their diet was mocked by the more flamboyant Royalists.

After Cromwell

Even without its Cromwell connection, the house has a fascinating past. In the 19th century it became an inn, the Cromwell Arms, and the front was rendered over. It was returned to its current half-timbered appearance in 1905 when it became home to the vicar of St Mary's. The local authority took over ownership in 1986. Although the house has gone through so many changes in its long life, it has now been successfully arranged to give an authentic flavour of how it looked when Cromwell lived here, and tells his story effectively.

The study as Cromwell might have known it

Through the city

Although the cathedral, Oliver Cromwell's House and the River Great Ouse waterside are what many visitors to Ely seek out, a further hour or two spent in the city, looking at other features of interest, makes for an even richer and more enjoyable experience.

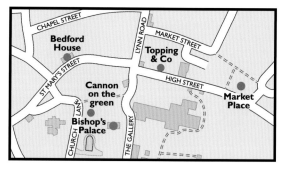

Cannon on the green

Between Oliver Cromwell's House and the west front of the cathedral is what may have been the village green of Ely's original settlement. Standing in the middle is a cannon. As close inspection will reveal, it is Russian, captured from the ruins of Sevastopol in 1855.
The taking of the naval port after a year-long siege brought an end to the Crimean War. Queen Victoria presented the gun to the city in 1860 after enough men had volunteered to allow the formation of the 6th Cambridgeshire Rifle Volunteer Corps at Ely.

Bishop's Palace

Bishop's Palace

Near the cathedral's west end is the former Bishop's Palace, a fine brick building much altered since it was entirely rebuilt by Bishop Alcock (see page 7) around 1490. It is thought that a gallery linked the palace to the south-west transept, its name surviving in the street running south from there. Bishop Laney (1667–75) undid most of Alcock's work, leaving only the two towers and creating the present three-sided court. Bishops of Ely lived in the palace until the early 20th century. During the Second World War it was a convalescent home for servicemen and afterwards for many years a school for children with physical disabilities. Since 1986 it has been a Sue Ryder Care home for the chronically sick.

A tawdry beginning

St Audrey was an alternative name for St Etheldreda, and in later centuries St Audrey's Fairs were held in May and October to commemorate her. Necklaces known as St Audrey's lace were sold, and by the 17th century became a byword for the cheap, flashy finery one would find at fairs like these – hence 'tawdry' goods.

Bedford House

On St Mary's Street, halfway between the Lamb Hotel and Oliver Cromwell's House, is elegant Bedford House, built around 1800 and identified by a large coat of arms over the doorway of its later single-storey extension. From the 1840s to the 1920s it was the headquarters of the Bedford Level Corporation, the body in charge of draining the Fens (see pages 24–25). Until 1968 it was still associated with drainage organizations. The motto beneath the coat of arms is *Arridet Aridum*, which means 'Dryness Pleaseth'.

Topping & Company

A unique treat in the High Street is a visit to bookseller Topping & Company. Pots of tea and coffee can be enjoyed by visitors browsing three floors of bookcases stacked high with a vast choice of literary delights, with views over the cathedral. Regular book signings take place here too.

Coat of arms over Bedford House

Quin Hollick's 'Ely Sundial'

Market Place

Market Place has always been the focus of activity for the people of the city. Week-long fairs were once held here (see panel opposite), livestock roamed here, and for centuries a weekly market has taken place – since 1801 on Thursdays. Once more cluttered with buildings, today's market place, when the stalls disappear, is at first sight just an open space. But look more carefully. Within the pavement are several fascinating additions, explained by nearby plaques. Quin Hollick's 'Ely Sundial' (2001) actually works. It also marks Ely's exact position on the world map. Surrounding stones commemorate aspects of the city's life, past and present.

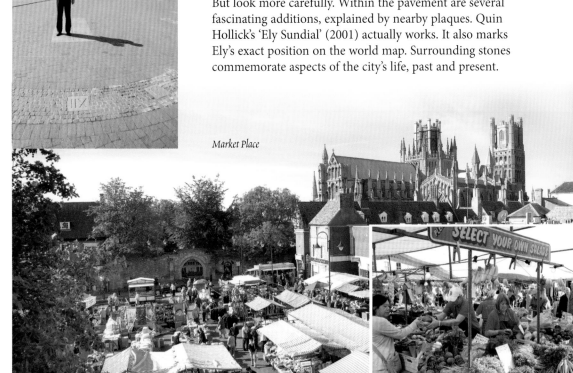

Market Place

Waterside

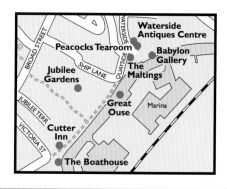

Part of the magic of a visit to Ely is exploring where the city's historic streets meet the River Great Ouse. Here, when the sun shines, weeping willow trees shade a rich variety of waterbirds, boats come and go and people wander along the riverside path – perhaps in search of antiques, a boat trip, or maybe to eat or drink by the water.

Wildlife

Waterbirds that you are almost certain to find by the river include Canada (and other) geese, mute swans, mallards and Muscovy ducks. Herons, too, visit at quieter times. Visitors are requested to feed them only in the slipway area near the Peacocks Tearoom, and only with the duck pellets available from The Maltings, as bread is bad for them.

Babylon Gallery

A local area's nickname is kept alive in this 'small but perfectly formed' riverside art gallery created from one of the many former breweries in the vicinity. It is a publicly funded professional gallery for contemporary visual art, and one of Ely's most popular visitor attractions. Babylon was actually a disreputable area of shipwrights, basketmakers, potters and eel-catchers on the far side of the river (where the marina now is). It was cut off from the rest of the town, first by the rerouting of the river *c.*1200 and further by the arrival of the railway in 1845.

Babylon Gallery

The Great Ouse

Ely's river, the Great Ouse, rises in Northamptonshire and flows 150 miles (240km) through many lovely and historic towns to enter The Wash at King's Lynn. Its course is followed by the scenic Ouse Valley Way footpath. The river played a vital part in the town's life, not only as a source of food and building materials but as an important trade route. It was via the Ouse 900 years ago that Barnack stone came from Northamptonshire to build the cathedral.

Waterside refreshments

There are lots of places in Ely to enjoy refreshments, but riverside is always special and they don't come more charming than Peacocks Tearoom. Although not open every day, this traditional tearoom has a wide choice of teas (more than 60) and delicious home-cooked treats – and if the weather is fine the garden is a delightful place to take tea and river-watch. For something a little stronger, and heartier meals, The Cutter Inn is a good choice, as is The Boathouse restaurant where you may even find local eel on the menu.

Waterside Antiques Centre

Like The Maltings below, this wonderful old brick building, full of exposed beams, is a former maltings, protected by a preservation order. Three floors provide a charming setting for more than 60 individual trade stands, making this East Anglia's largest centre for antiques and collectables.

Waterside Antiques Centre

'Lincolnshire Limestone' in Jubilee Gardens

The Maltings

Malt, with hops, sugar and yeast, is an ingredient of traditional English beer. In this building, now a public hall, cinema and restaurant, locally grown barley was processed into malt. Built in 1868 by Ebenezer Harlock as part of his brewery, The Maltings were badly damaged by fire in 1967, and later sold for £100 to East Cambridgeshire Council by the owners, Watney Mann. In the foyer, where barley was once sifted and dried, is the Ely Ribe Tapestry, designed and woven in Denmark, celebrating the city's links with its twin cathedral city of Ribe.

The Maltings

Jubilee Gardens

This attractive park, between the Ouse and Broad Street, was for centuries part of Ely's biggest commercial area. Here, along channels cut in from the river, barges loaded and unloaded, servicing the warehouses and workshops that crowded round: timber yards, tanning pits, potteries, breweries, basketmakers and more. Saved from development by local people, it is now a delightful area in which to stroll and sit (or play, if you're a child). Features include the *Yellow Eel* (see page 23), the steel *Eel* by Peter Baker (2006; see page 22) and the huge *Lincolnshire Limestone* water feature celebrating the importance of the waterway network to the Isle of Ely.

Eel Trail

Ely's Eel Trail, created in 2004 and waymarked by bronze eels in the pavement, celebrates past and present: the past in Ely's rich heritage of buildings and water-based activity; the present in modern works of art along the way. The original artworks, mainly by Elizabeth-Jane Grose, all relate to eels: how they grow, how they look, how to catch them, how to cook them!

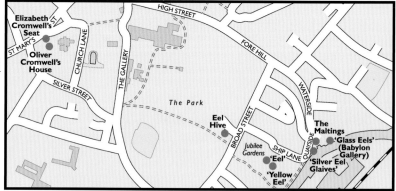

The modern 'Eel' by Peter Baker on the Eel Trail

Silver Eel Glaives

Near The Maltings (see page 21) is a sculpture based on eel glaives, the metal knives to be seen in the Ely Museum (see pages 12–13). As long ago as Anglo-Saxon days, fishermen stood on the tops of dykes hurling the glaives into the ditches, harpoon-like, hoping to ensnare an eel lurking on the muddy bottom. The eight blades, made by local blacksmiths, reflect Ely Cathedral's famous octagon (see page 6).

Glass Eels

Five engraved glass panels form part of the entrance to the Babylon Gallery (see page 20). They represent stages in the dramatic life of the European eel: spawning in the Sargasso Sea near Bermuda; swimming thousands of miles to European waters; maturing in inland waterways before returning to the Sargasso to spawn and die.

Elizabeth-Jane Grose

The artist responsible for the features on the Eel Trail has carried out several important commissions in a variety of media both in the UK and Europe. Elizabeth-Jane Grose lives and works in a rural setting, specializing in art works closely related to the sites they inhabit. In particular, she explores the relationship between people and their natural environment, looking to make use of natural and sustainable materials.

'Glass Eels' at entrance to Babylon Gallery

On the Eel Trail

'Eel Hive' in The Park

Elizabeth Cromwell's seat

Elizabeth Cromwell's seat

The motif on this seat is a uniquely presented recipe telling how to roast eels. Appropriately it is one of Elizabeth Cromwell's own recipes. The seat surrounds a purple-leafed plum tree outside Cromwell's House (see pages 16–17).

Eel Hive

The 'hives' were eel traps, small 'tunnels' of soaked, split rods of willow left in rivers overnight, into which unsuspecting eels would swim and be snared. This willow sculpture, based on the shape of a hive, stands at the start of the climb back through the park to the cathedral and city centre. Like the glaives, actual eel traps can be seen in Ely Museum.

Yellow Eel

This mosaic eel, which seems to be making its way down to the river, is made from fragments of pottery found during excavations at Jubilee Gardens by Cambridge archaeologists working with television's *Time Team* in 2000. Yellow eels are, confusingly, not necessarily yellow. Rather, the description refers to the immature adult stage of development, which might also result in a green, brown or grey colour.

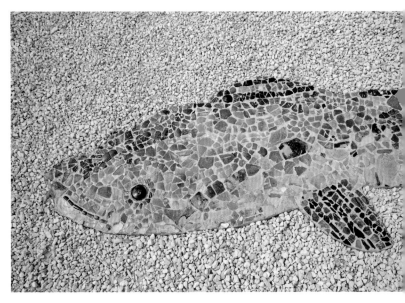

'Yellow Eel'

The Fens

Until a few hundred years ago the Fens were a huge, flat marshy wilderness, stretching away in every direction from Ely, which was protected on its isle by rock capped with clay and gravel. Today only a small area of natural fen remains. The rest has been systematically drained to create some of England's richest farmland – but only at the price of many livelihoods. No visit to Ely would be complete without some understanding of the surrounding Fens; this guide explains something of their history and highlights some interesting Fenland (and other) places to visit.

Wicken Fen

Wicken Fen

As one of the last remaining areas of natural Fenland, Wicken Fen, near Soham and 5 miles (8 kilometres) south-east of Ely, is one of Britain's oldest and most visited nature reserves. Here, unthreatened by human intervention, wildlife of all sorts thrives. Mammal species are measured in dozens, bird species in hundreds and insect species in thousands. Sedge is harvested for thatching in the traditional way. Wicken Fen is punctuated by lodes (ancient drains) and droves (ancient paths) along which you can walk for miles to access the hides and habitats. The rebuilt wooden wind pump here illustrates an early response to the problem of shrinking land (see the panel opposite).

Welney Wetland Centre

Run by the Wildfowl & Wetlands Trust, this 1,000-acre (400-ha) reserve, 10 miles (16 kilometres) north of Ely, is part of the Ouse Washes, a flood storage reservoir sandwiched between Vermuyden's Old and New Bedford rivers (see panel). During the year, the reserve is host to thousands of migrating birds, and it is also the habitat of many wetland plants, flowers and creatures. The superb visitor centre with cafés adds another dimension to the visit, which is an absolute must for nature lovers.

Welney Wetland Centre

Stretham Old Engine

As the land shrank, the rotating scoops powered by windmills were insufficient to lift rainwater from the fields – sometimes 19 feet (6 metres) below the drains. An intermediate channel might double the lift, but this, too, became inadequate. Fortunately, steam arrived, six times more powerful. The Old Engine at Stretham, 4 miles (6.5 kilometres) south of Ely, was once one of more than 100 beam engines which paddled the water slowly but effectively into the Old West River and safely away to The Wash. It is now open to visitors on certain days of the year.

Prickwillow Drainage Engine Museum

Eventually scoop wheels, however powered, became ineffective in many areas. In those places, conventional pumps were introduced, driven by more powerful horizontal steam engines. In the 1920s, diesel engines began to be installed, often with the old steam plant remaining as a standby. At Prickwillow, 4 miles (7 kilometres) east of Ely, the diesel engine has been magnificently preserved and has now been joined by other Fenland drainage engines. Electrical pumping still goes on at the plant next door to the museum, which is open several days a week in summer.

Cornelius Vermuyden

Drainage had gone on since Roman times, but it was only after 1630 that the landscape really changed. Then, the 4th Earl of Bedford and his fellow 'Adventurers' (see page 12), wanting to farm the rich black peat beneath the Fens, employed Dutch engineer Cornelius Vermuyden to build huge drains to take away the water. This ended the livelihood of many 'Fen tigers' (see page 3) but did indeed provide fertile farming. However, what Bedford's men failed to anticipate was that the peat would shrink and the land would drop by 'the height of a man in the life of a man' – well below the level of the drains. As water doesn't flow uphill, and to preserve the farmland, increasingly powerful pumping solutions have been needed.

Denver Sluice

The massive sluice gates you can see at Denver, 15 miles (25 kilometres) north of Ely, are the epicentre of Fenland drainage. Cornelius Vermuyden (see panel below) dug the 'Old Bedford River', a straight cut from Earith to the tidal Ouse reducing the distance to the sea by 10 miles (16 kilometres). Later, a second cut, the 'New Bedford River' was made. The two channels converge on Denver where huge gates control water going in and out of the Great Ouse, effectively preventing backflow from the tides on to the farmland below. The many boats, the working windmill and the popular pub make it an area now visited by numerous tourists.

Prickwillow Drainage Engine Museum

PRICKWILLOW
DRAINAGE ENGINE
MUSEUM

Towards Newmarket

Anyone leaving Ely's 'isle' has a rich choice of wildlife and Fenland locations to visit (see pages 24–25) and, within a relatively short drive, there are also attractive places that reflect more varied interests.

Burwell

Once a wealthy inland port, attractive Burwell is well worth exploration. Its grand 15th-century church, St Mary's, designed by the architect of King's College, Cambridge, is one of the finest medieval buildings in East Anglia. Burwell's 'edge of the Fens' location, 10 miles (16 kilometres) south of Ely, has resulted in a charming and exceptional museum exploring how life in the Fens was once lived. Set in reconstructed historic buildings by a restored windmill, it has displays including farm machinery, a blacksmith's shop, a Nissen hut with wartime memorabilia, vintage vehicles . . . the list goes on. Opening times tend to be restricted, so you are advised to check before visiting.

Newmarket statue

Newmarket Experience

Newmarket, 13.5 miles (22 kilometres) south-east of Ely, is the world home of horse racing. Apart from many training establishments, including the British Racing School, and the famous races themselves on the town's heath, there are many other equine institutions to interest the visitor. The comprehensive way to see it all is to take the Newmarket Experience tour which encompasses watching horses at the gallops, the National Stud, the National Horseracing Museum (with much to interest non-horsey people, and a splendid area for children) and a visit to a training yard, racing school or Tattersalls Bloodstock Sales ring.

SWAFFHAM PRIOR

Devil's Dyke

Devil's Dyke

Between Burwell and Swaffham Prior, and 11 miles (18 kilometres) from Ely, runs Devil's Dyke, a defensive ditch and rampart thought to be Britain's finest Anglo-Saxon earthwork. It stretches 7.5 miles (12 kilometres) across open chalkland between what was impassable Fenland to the north and impenetrable woodland to the south. Built *c.* AD 600 by the East Angles, its aim was to keep out the Britons from further west. Today it is a rich grassland habitat of wild flowers, herbs, butterflies and other insects. Although much of the dyke is privately owned, there is a public footpath running along its whole length.

Wicken Corn Windmill

Wicken Corn Windmill

Near Wicken Fen (see page 24) is the village's ancient corn mill, restored and working. The millers are happy to extend a personal welcome and to demonstrate how flour was ground in the old days. It is an especially valuable experience for children who think that flour originates in the bag.

Swaffham-Two-Churches

Near Burwell is the village of Swaffham Prior, distinctive for its two churches in one churchyard. Both of them have octagonal towers, and both originate from the 12th century. St Mary's is now the parish church, and contains fascinating windows depicting scenes from the First World War. St Cyriac's is preserved empty and has amazing acoustics. It is used occasionally for exhibitions.

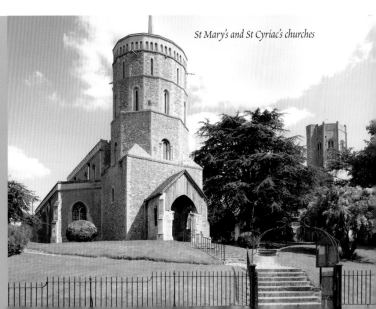
St Mary's and St Cyriac's churches

Beyond Ely

Visiting the places mentioned here ties in easily with other places of interest in the area. Denny Abbey is on the way to Cambridge, Anglesey Abbey is near Wicken, Burwell and Swaffham Prior (see pages 26–27), while the few minutes' drive between March and Welney (see page 24) is a true Fenland experience. Huntingdon is ideal for Cromwell devotees, while St Ives, just to its east, has wider appeal.

Church of St Wendreda, March

Carved angel, St Wendreda's Church

St Wendreda's Church, March

March lies a few miles north-east of Ely on another 'island' of the Fens. It was once a big railway town and Sir John Betjeman described one of its churches, St Wendreda's, as 'worth cycling 40 miles in a headwind to see'. St Wendreda was a Saxon princess and sister to Ely's St Etheldreda. The church is world-famous for its 16th-century double-hammerbeam 'Angel Roof' featuring 120 carved angels as well as saints and martyrs. Its font dates from the Norman era. During the week, the key is held at the Star Inn nearby.

Recalling RAF Witchford

In its three-year life during the Second World War, RAF Witchford, now a business park, echoed to the roar of Wellington, Stirling and Lancaster bombers going to and coming from raids over Germany. A fascinating tiny museum commemorates the men, many of them New Zealanders, who flew from here and from nearby Mepal. The museum is in the offices of Grovemere Holdings, in the business park off the A142.

Anglesey Abbey

Anglesey Abbey

Huttleston Broughton, 1st Lord Fairhaven, remodelled this country house – a former priory, 10 miles (16 kilometres) south of Ely – to preserve what is virtually a bygone way of life: that of a 20th-century gentleman's country residence. On his death in 1966 he left it to the National Trust. The house is filled with sumptuous furnishings and rare works of art, the collection of clocks being especially renowned. Around the house stretch wonderful lawns and parkland, full of delightful surprises: wonderful avenues, hidden glades, a riverside walk, all adorned by a huge variety of statues – mythical beasts, Roman emperors and Greek gods among them.

Cromwell Museum, Huntingdon

Oliver Cromwell was born in Huntingdon and represented the town in Parliament. Hidden amid its pedestrianized streets is the Cromwell Museum, housed in an 800-year-old building, once the school that the sometime Lord Protector attended. The museum's rich collection includes many portraits and objects relating to Cromwell, and for those who are interested in this period of history coming here and going to St Ives represents a perfect complement to visiting his house in Ely.

Farmland Museum, Denny Abbey

On the A10 between Ely and Cambridge, this museum is popular with families. The collections recall farming and rural crafts through the ages, with agricultural machinery and reconstructions of bygone countryside dwellings.

Norris Museum, St Ives

The charming, unspoiled market town of St Ives is another place with Cromwell connections – his home in the 1630s; his fine statue stands in the town centre. The Norris Museum, in its 1930s chapel-like building, tells the story of the former county of Huntingdonshire through a wide variety of artefacts and paintings. The museum also has a unique collection of ice skates!

St Ives

Information

i **Tourist Information Centre**
29 St Mary's Street, Ely,
Cambridgeshire CB7 4HF
tel: 01353 662062
email: tic@eastcambs.gov.uk
website: www.visitely.org.uk

Shopmobility
For the use of wheelchairs and powered scooters
for those with limited mobility.
Based at Ely Museum, Market Street
Thurs–Sat 10.30–13.00 and 14.00–16.00
To book, tel: 01353 666655

Tours and Trips
Information on a variety of pre-bookable tours
and trips can be obtained from the Tourist
Information Centre.

Ely area attractions
Anglesey Abbey 01223 810080,
www.nationaltrust.org.uk/angleseyabbey;
Babylon Gallery 01353 669022,
www.babylongallery.co.uk;
The Boathouse Restaurant 01353 664388,
www.cambscuisine.com/The Boathouse;
Burwell Museum 01638 605544,
www.burwellmuseum-org-uk-.ik.com;
Cromwell Museum, Huntingdon 01480 375830,
www.cambridgeshire.gov.uk/cromwell;
The Cutter Inn 01353 662713,
www.thecutterinn.co.uk;
Ely Cathedral 01353 667735,
www.cathedral.ely.anglican.org;
Ely Museum 01353 666655,
www.elymuseum.org.uk;
Farmland Museum, Denny Abbey
01223 860988,
www.dennyfarmlandmuseum.org.uk;
The Maltings 01353 662633,
www.themaltingsely.com;
National Horseracing Museum 01638 667333,
www.nhrm.co.uk;
National Stud 01638 666789,
www.nationalstud.co.uk;

Newmarket Experience 01638 667200,
www.newmarketexperience.co.uk;
Norris Museum, St Ives 01480 497314,
www.norrismuseum.org.uk;
Oliver Cromwell's House 01353 662062,
www.olivercromwellshouse.co.uk;
Peacocks Tearoom 01353 661100
www.peacockstearoom.co.uk;
Prickwillow Drainage Engine Museum
01353 688360,
www.prickwillow-engine-museum.co.uk;
St Wendreda's Church, March
01354 653377, www.stwendreda.co.uk;
Stained Glass Museum 01353 660347,
www.stainedglassmuseum.com;
Stretham Old Engine 01353 648578,
www.strethamoldengine.org.uk;
Waterside Antiques Centre 01353 667066,
www.ely.org.uk/waterside.html;
Topping & Company Booksellers 01353 645005,
www.toppingbooks.co.uk;
Welney Wetland Centre 01353 860711,
www.wwt.org.uk/visit/welney;
Wicken Corn Windmill 01664 822751
or 01628 782946,
www.geocities.com/wickenmill;
Wicken Fen 01353 720274,
www.nationaltrust.org.uk/wickenfen

Sacrist's Gate

Index of attractions

Welney Wetland Centre

'The Virgin Mary' by David Wynne,
Ely Cathedral

Topping &
Company
Booksellers

Front cover main: Bishop's Palace and Ely Cathedral; top l to r: Oliver Cromwell's House, Eel Trail mosaic, waterfowl on the River Great Ouse
Back cover: Boating on the River Great Ouse

Peacocks Tearoom

Acknowledgements

Photography © Pitkin Publishing by Neil Jinkerson except 14–15 (Heather Hook), 31c and ibc bl (Peter Smith/Newbery Smith Photography). Additional photography by kind permission of: Alamy 6 (Robert Stainfork), 29b (Holmes Garden Photos); East Cambridgeshire District Council (Geoff Durrant) 17t; FotoLibra (David Young) 29t; John McIlwain fc tr, 13tr, 21c, 23tr, 31t, 26t, 27c; George Peacock 32; Hugh Topping 31b.

The publishers would like to thank Mike Petty of the *Cambridge Evening News* and people from the organizations mentioned in the text for their assistance in the preparation of the guide.

Written by John McIlwain; the author has asserted his moral rights.
Edited by Marilynne Lanng of Bookwork.
Designed by Glad Stockdale.
Additional picture research by Marilynne Lanng of Bookwork.

Maps by The Map Studio, Romsey, Hants, UK. Based on Mapvu10 mapping produced by Lovell Johns Ltd. Generated from Ordnance Survey digital data with the permission of The Controller of Her Majesty's Stationery Office © Crown Copyright. Licence number 43368U.

Publication in this form © Pitkin Publishing 2010.

All information correct at time of going to press, but may be subject to change.

Printed in Great Britain.
ISBN 978-1-84165-214-6   1/10

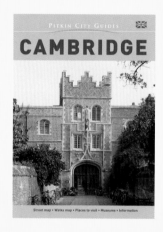
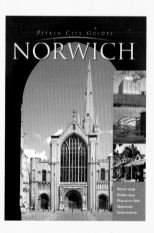